ARACHNID

COURTNEY WALLACE

For my closest friends;
The Good Egg Basket, my OG's Since the 90's, my American
friends, my MK Besties, "Dolphie", L Bizzle crew, and
Welshies.

For my family, who believe in me every day.

ARACHNID

Contents

I

Fortify

GIANTS

To stand so tall, over a sea of the defenceless
They know no better
They know only here
In the dirt
A blood stain on the hands of a Messiah
They crawl, they endure
While the Giants reign, and while minds rapture
Falling to their doom
In red satin and false promises
What good are wings that wither
That fall like Icarus, and land among the glorious dead
If only

The sky opened up and swallowed whole the tyrants
Dressed in white
With roses for hands
Only then might we save the souls of the silent
And as we endure the night
Over hushed screams, and lost ambitions
Might we deliver salvation

CRYSTALISE

Unravel my aching frame, and lay me bare
For I know not the softness of love
Until now, it taketh
Scorning me
But perhaps, in this moment
It leadeth me
Deeper into your eyes, your breath
I know not what is safe, I know not what is sheltered
But my fibres clench and entwine
Until I succumb to you, in all manner of being
Each vein collapsing
Unveiling the bruising of my structure
Every sin becomes holy, every shadow a painting
If I am to be taken again
Into a Hellish inferno
I wish for the pain to stain me
To block out sense, and empty my skull of tragedy
For only then will I remember my humanity
For only then will it crystallise
And I with it

ON THIS HILL

So, die on it
This mound of chaos and destruction
Of resentment and power
There is no love in thee
Only hatred that spews from the tongue and cheek
Into the heart of whom you sought to dissolve
Until there is nothing left but ash
A black stain upon your hands
A remanence of what once was

GUNPOWDER

I understand now
That my words carved consequence
Newfangled
That I pressed when I should have pulled
Oh, the joy you bring
The fireworks that fill my sky
The smell of gunpowder
Had I not been a fool
Had I waited for you
To fall as I had fallen
Perhaps we would know more of each other
Enough to break the silence
Molded by our temperament

OUTLAW

It is the menace that bringeth change
For screaming silently is still heard
When the deaf come to listen
And the wolves come to bawl

IT ALL STEMS FROM

Dance upon me
To remind ourselves of better days
Childhood dreams
And prepubescence
Contagious smiles
Doltish nescience
Without worry
Only nightmares from that we'd wake
And be reminded that we are safe
We did not fear the Reaper
For death be an eternity away
We'd find friends under logs
And on pub climbing frames
Never to be seen again
Never to remember their names
But it mattered not
For life was an adventure
That we got to have every day
Always in the moment
Always a chance to frolic
In a story we'd create
Oh, to be young again
And cherish naivety

SANCTUARY

Under love's dome
I fear the outer world
For it rips at my skin
And forms under its nail beds
Its silence mocks me
Yet I am safe in this temple
Build on ash and persistence
Let us stay in our safety
Making claim to our sanctuary

PAPER CUT

I gave my all to the idea
That someone might just love me
And when I had nothing left
I was forgotten in the dirt
Black and blue
Bleeding underneath the mask
One, two, three
Until I was covered, head to toe
In a thousand tiny cuts
Each one, a word or gesture
That fragmented my heart
More than the last
And I only hate you now
For robbing me of sense
When the lies banged on the gates
They persisted with the truth
That all I had
Was an empty throne room
And my own blood on my fingertips
For each brick I laid
Another crumbled
Until all that was left was a pile of rubble
And my cold dead heart

ÓÐR

From the future, from the past
Challenge my soul
Until I'm worthy
May lightning strike
May death unite me
With the glory of the Old Ways
Draupnir
Mjölnir
Gungnir
Surtr
Pledge my hands to the hilt
For they are no longer mine

KINGDOM OF RUIN

Show me that you're better off
And I will take my leave
For there be nothing worse
Than the feeling of loneliness in your own domain
You'd have me branded as ludicrous
Farcical
When I only rule with good intent
I have slain my thoughts
A hundred times over
On the battlefield of perfidy
Only to be reincarnated
As a foot soldier
Charging into narcissistic conflicts
Against my will
Against my laws
The Heavens beat down with drums and might
Give me strength
To wage war on this Hell
A Trojan Horse
Filled with every tormenting word
Curses of a hundred shamans
I bare the mark of Heathen
So take up your sword
And I will smite thee down

With one swift blow
Cuing the final curtain call

PIROUETTE

Do you know not what you do
When you hold me by the waist
And spin me round
Pirouetting with two left feet
How I fall
Within your gaze
Your charm
You balance me in your palm
Making time stand still
Just like in movies
Except we get it wrong
We laugh
At our perfectly imperfect choreography
While rehearsing in the rain

FATE

You hold the keys to my fate
For I know not the path I tread
The river flows in ways unknown to me
Yet I stumble in the hopes
That you will be kind
That you will be merciful

KILL THE KING

You flooded the pages of your own story
Until the ink ran dry and it started to crack
Washing away the victories in one swift tempest
And all that you were with it

How can you stand being so tall
When there's nothing left to see
My feet took me away
From the ocean to the trees
As you looked out towards the sea
I became nothing

How can you stand being so small
When there's branches above your head
Blocking the Sun and Moon
And towering black spires
Making day and night look the same
From the hovel of your castle

CINDER

Use the ash to paint your story
Rewrite your repertoire
Before the pages burn away
Catastrophise your Shangri La

BULLY

I can hear them now
They mock me
Turn the knife buried in my stomach
Fracturing all of my being
But I am not afraid

BREW

Stewed in murky pools
Caked in residue
I feel the endorphins
Move around my body
Like mellow tides
Riding on the smell of new books
And old dreams

SERVITUDE

My pain is a project
My pulse the enemy
Revoke my will
And all that's within me
For one more night
In your sweet company
I'd give my all
For your eternity

TANK

Banging on the glass
Screaming into the water
Pocketed in each bubble
Is my urgency
But you cannot hear
Over muffled whimpers
My desperation
As I run out of breath

FIRST OF MANY

I'm clutching at your words
Like they're strings attached to my throat
Pulling on my vocal chords
But nothing comes out
You leave me with a puddle of thoughts
To swallow up in the night
And a longing in my chest
For the days that are empty
A tugging on my lungs
From when you stole my breath
And you said I was beautiful

II

Chistle

L'EXQUISITE DOULEUR

Could it be
That your forbidden touch, so far from reach
Has managed to rest its hand upon my head
Stretched out, winding
Yet I cannot tear myself from this paradoxical pilgrimage
Fated to only end in catharsis
Bent on the hope of "if" and "when"
I hear your name on the breeze
It melts on my tongue
And plays in my diaphragm
Using my rib cage like ivory keys

SCRATCH

What did I do
To carry these scars
Medals of misery
They lay upon me
Refractions of destitution
Calluses on my soul
Unlovable, unthinkable grief
Maybe someone will see these bones
And resurrect them
Fuel this pyre with hatred and dispute
And discard all else
For the sake of taciturnity

HEAVY

My heart is full of stones
It aches
It tires
Silently straining in the depths of my chest
It beckons
Will there be no relief?
No warmth, no comfort
Captivated by a darkness, it'll surely rot away
Until all that is left are the rocks and sorrow that torment it

GUILT

I felt it stab like knives, deep within my chest
Icicles stretching into my tissue, and spreading like spores
I see your face, exhausted, glaze over in defeat
I shudder, knowing I am its architect
Each part of me breaks down like tumble blocks
Snapping the fibres that hold me
I lay bare
Swollen
Catatonic
The shards splinter into my vertebrae
Convulsing all that I am
Melting through my tear ducts and engulfing all my sense

SORROW

It's exhausting
To cry so loud
And have no one answer
I suppose that's why
The darkness seems so warm
When it's freezing in the light
As your heart sits in a pit
Within your rib cage, a chamber of disarray
A pool of sorrow
Festering the anguish
Oh to be loved
Oh to be free

EMBERS

Tell me all your secrets so I can set them alight
I'll watch the embers flicker in my shadow
Feeling blessed for the depression
Await the sunrise of tomorrow

WORTHLESS

And as I sought comfort I was met with shame
That I was worthless and undeserving
That your presence should humble me
And I should shower you in gold
When my waters ran red
And my tears ran cold
The edge never felt so much like home

CATHEDRAL

I watch you from afar
Under the arches of God
You breathe in time with my lungs
Eyes of the ocean
I have begun the descent
My love is stained glass
Rose tinted and vibrant
I pray
If only you could see
You are the Cherub's song
The Holy Grail
You are the candles lit in prayer
And the tabernacle of my heart

SPIT

I am left alone, half alive
If I die
Would you bury me
With all our hate
These wounds are my trinkets
They decorate me
In all my failed attempts
Plagued by a yearning heart
A burden
To be wanted
But I believe you'd laugh
As I lay in the street
Among the rats
While you lay among the stars

BITTER

You taste so bitter when you speak
Every remark, every bite
I sense it in your words
As they crunch down on my throat
And you gorge
When you snap back
Bawl
It breaks down my ambition
It stings inside my chest
A venom coursing through
From vein to spit
Leaving me in pieces
As the enzymes tear me asunder

THINGS

If I had the lungs I'd breathe
If I had the mouth I'd sing
But I exist silently
And marvel only at those that can do such things

WAGE WAR

You waged a war within my chest
The battle scars dressed up like uniform
Poisoned by the soldiers in my dopamine
Half in the war paint of my veins
Half in shackles
I'm not okay
But, for you, that wasn't enough
You broke the dam
Instead of making amends
To try and try again
Only to watch me suffer
As I waited on your empty promises
But it's okay
I'm stronger now
And I see right through
I won't try again
I've erupted anew
Removing the knife
And every sense of you
For I no longer wait
For you to say I'm worthy

FABRICATE

Run into my pain, relapsing
You overdosed on something sinister
Until the walls dripped black
And the sky turned grey
I heard the whispers convulsing
Under pretences and dotted lines
Don't come crying to me
When the paintings start to talk
They'll only mock and feed
Upon the rise of your last dawn

HANGMAN

Over the sink, you hang your head
Noose woven from plaits and pigtails
The mirror mocks a little harder
From bathroom stalls and viscous daydreams
Target practice for jealous eyes
Pen and paper letter games
Built from cruel intentions
You are afraid

ELSEWHERE

I see the reflection in your eyes
But it isn't of here
They blink away all that we built
To make way for something new
Did it really mean so little to you

What made you so cold
Past mistakes take hold of your heart
Now it rots in the light
And there are no stars in the night sky

Was it so hard to ascend with me
When I burnt paychecks with your spirit
Love is gasoline
Choking on the fumes
And reconstructing theorems

I appeased your Gods before considering mine
Yet time still took from me
All that I ever had
And all that I ever will be

CHASING DIAMONDS

Salt and pepper
Won't heal wounds so deep
There's rot in your cavities
And defeat in your eyes
You chase diamonds
Like they'll soothe your soul
But they are tougher than iron
Buried
Betrothed
You long for the satin
The new, the blue
Yet you borrow only frailty
Masking truth with hymns and storybook men

HEAVY IS THE HEAD

Everybody knows someone's own worst enemy
So keep your black book tucked away in your nightstand
Because family values are built on piousy
And false prophets are the ones who watch over us
Tell me again of your sorrow and pride
That your prayers bring rain
Tell me how your nights of kneeling
Don't stop the damp soaking your feet
And that you hunger with a full plate
Heavy is the head that wears the crown
But heavier be the hands that wield
What say you, sword or serenades
To the empty chapel, that is God's waiting room

SYNAPSES

All I wanted was some air to breathe
But your bitterness seeped in when you were angry
Face dissolved by landed punches
Made for enemies
Blissful language turned sour
We dance with clenched fists
Face as red as the flag you carry
Smashed up glass and chipped door frames
Who taught you how to hate
Because that's all you did for me

FREEWAY

I wanted peace of mind
But instead you took pieces of it
I craved the way it tastes
The way it exhilarates
Another casualty
Thrown from the back seat
Forever chasing sunlight
Pain drives a Porsche
And I fuel mistakes
Always missing the stop lights
When you were showing red
Now I'm cut up and numb
Call 911

ONE DAY

One day
He might feel the tide eloping his heart
Burrowing in his veins
And casting a shadow over all pain
And I will hold out for that horizon
With hope in my own heart
And trust in my veins
And yearning in my mind

I plead for the words to fall from his lips
So that I may bask in their light
I hope for them to stain me
And dance in my dreams
A feeling I have felt for yonder
A craving my soul desires

But though my ears seeketh such discourse
I will wait a thousand nights
If it means they are untainted
That they humbly find me
And take me in their clutches
To be cherished
To be loved

HEROIN CHIC

Cocaine chem trails
Class A deities
Runway treadmills
And cast out reveries
Don't eat, don't sleep
Substance therapy
Vape meals, trade deals
When the mirror is the enemy

ETHANOL SYNDROME

Hit a girl with a smile
When you want to use your fists
Make her stay a while
Just to see where she fits
Vile dreams, thick jeans
You believe in the afterlife
She's looking for her Pisces
You're looking for her bra wire
Built on homemade remedies
Is this the one solution
To your own self liberty

BLEED

I am clutching the stem of a rose
And now my fingers bleed
Is it love, to let go
And exist in sweet misery

GRIEVANCE

I grieve that which has not yet passed
Prolonging my suffering
In the hopes that I will find comfort
In the tears and torment
Maybe the sorrow will turn to stone
Or maybe I will be engulfed
In whatever fire lay waiting

III

Triatominae

SOIL

As I fall from grace, and all manner of humanity
I wish for only you to guide me back to the ground
For the soil to collect at my feet
And in that moment, we create eternity
And in that moment, we birth ardour

DRAGONFLY

From ashes grew roots that engulfed the dark
And tore apart nightmares
They uttered defiance and bloomed among the weeds
As though their strength surpassed giants
They bore exultancy and cunning
While rotting the perverse
And as the dark began to shed
Like beacons hatching from cocoons
A hopefulness bled into the soil

All the while, resteth azure
Emerging from their own plight
Rustling into life
And fluttering from their slumber
Sprouting a magnificence, unbound
Ready to live
Ready to fly

WEB

Pearls sit upon the threads which cling to the foliage
A collection of jewels that hold and rotate the world
Each row laced with an abundance of dewy gems
Marvelling at the Sun in a plentiful cluster

Trees gorge on the moisture
That grasps firmly onto each leaf
Small and nimble
Perfectly balancing crystal balls along them
Like tight rope walkers and fortune tellers
Conducted by the eight-legged freaks that run them

CHRYSALIS

Bloom the blades that cut so deep
And leadeth me away
For I shudder now at the dirt
Which gathers beneath my feet
And ripples with anguish
Mycelium feeds the ground with my fear
It learns
It nourishes
As I become one with the World that once tormented me
I give all to Her
As I take root, and settle among the trees
She basks in the gift of flesh, and I rot away in daydreams of
better days
Blood feeds friends
And I birth anew
My radicles sprouting six feet deep
And reaching towards the stars

FIREFLIES

Street lamps light my way
Through city streets and disarray
Like pebbles above my head
They guide me towards my homestead
They keep me from the demons
Like fireflies or mountain beacons
Until I safely walk through my front door
Until I venture back once more

FOR WHEN THE TULIPS WITHER

The flutters of my heart spoke to me
They whispered your name, among sweet nothings
I captured your scent, your smile
And as the tulips withered, I began to know you
Framed in hands and butterflies
In new hellos and hard goodbyes
I presented you with golden flowers
In the hopes
That you might come to love me

MEADOWS

I never realised how soft the grass was
Until I had to lay in it
Oh what a dream life is
To be cradled in Earth's tendrils
Creating craters in meadows
Like rabbit holes from past pleasures

THE ORCHARD MANTIS

Vertex vexed
Flesh stuck in my teeth
I'm a winged insect
With cleavers underneath
Breathe in my humidity
As I pull you under
Deception served sweet
While I tear you asunder

TREES

It is in the embrace of trees
That I find my way
Disrupting the machine
That I serve only as a fixture
My lungs filled with fumes
And my veins a commuting tar
I pull away
And find them
The sky boarded up by canopies
They keep me dry
They keep me calm
These colossal friends
Rooted to me
Belonging to them
One day, to return

IN BLOOM

And how does the air taste
Around your neck
As your eyes linger on the flesh of one not so your own
The skeletal structure of an enemy
That has grown only from the depths of my heart and despair
The flower no longer buds in your presence
It only sheds
Until there is nothing left but a memory of itself in bloom
And yet
The thorns remain
They wrap around my wrists
A tendril bouquet, now love's graveyard
Yet you remain unscathed
Unaware and ignorant
That you watered the mud in which they grew
Flower bed to death bed
I utter no forgiveness
Only shame
Only resentment
That I would not be enough
I thought your heart gentle
Yet it stirs and echoes in chaos
I wish I had pressed harder on the walls
That instead of wood they were iron
That instead of hushed talks, they were bellows

So that I could flood the moat and burn the bridge
Before we got to it

I wither
Back into my dark sanctuary
Where I may lay myself to rest
Knowing that love may never find me
For I no longer seek it
And as my heart bleeds, encased in spicule
I recall the elation and the abhor
Watching you from my soul's window
Discarding my words and my embrace
In one swift gaze
And in that moment, I knew we were lost

RAIN

Specks flick onto my skin
They build and wash away the grit
Nails filled with evidence of clawing at the ground
And yet peace is neighbouring
I hear it
The dissolving of my fear
Of my hate
The dam decays
Through the soft aggression
It pours and joins its brethren
Washing away the dirt

WILD FLOWERS

I am terrified
You will be disappointed
And regretful
If you seek wild flowers
For I am a rose
My roots grow vast
My thorns sharp
And my petals vibrant
Sprouting from my pores
Are the saplings of my dreams

IN DIRT, WE BLOSSOM

The darkness is here
It knows my name
It calls to me
And dances on my brain

I tried to soak
But my skin only burns
A flower blooms in blood
Among the dirt and the ferns

AND

When we're together it feels like my hands are pressing piano
keys
Your skin feels like home, and mine smells like sweat
I see the ocean in your eyes, and as I cup your smile in my
palm
It feels like I'm holding God

I would walk to the ends of the Earth if you asked me to
I would jump
And I would clench your hand
As we dove into the lapsing waves

I hear you in my dreams, drumming on my heart
In the late morning, I see into you
Your breath on my neck, as the steam dances from our cups

The bed sheets are cool, speckled with perspiration and love
I understand why my tongue dances behind my teeth
Why I'd scream your name in a crowded room
If I died today
I'd know at least I did one thing right

And I would do it for a thousand years more
Passed the last dawn
I would still be yours

WAKE

My abdomen is filled with flies
They lay doubt in my stomach
I churn out frustration
And give birth to a monster
But I do not empty
They manifest
Sprouting endless larvae in my ligaments
My eyes secrete screams
While they're buzzing around in my skull

NUCLEUS

Is it you
Calling me home
While I dance drunkenly in the living room
That smile, that laugh
Reminding me of our past lives
Once again, finding me
You know all of my names
You know all of my aches
And soothe me in the moonlight
You show me your teeth, and I show you my claws
And we'll find where the susceptibility subsides

PARASITE

Keep me in your company
And choke the words out of my throat
My teeth turn to chess pieces
Your body, I am devote

CENTIPEDE

Fear the quiet
For that is where I reside
Rigorous
Sadistic
Venom in my system
Phobias written in my honour
Unravelling your confidence
For it is my nature to be so violent

ROT

Don't you see
I want it to hurt
I want to feel you when I'm face down in the dirt
I have ambition
That you will bite down
And taste how sweet I am on the inside
You asked me how I knew
And it was in the mirror I saw
The untameable
The whore
Awaiting the worthy
To take me in the dark
To own me
And make me your everything

TIDE

Hold me, for I cannot swim
I leave footprints in the sand
As I march towards the tide
It beckons me
To a home unknown
To an empty love that cannot recite
Here, it is cold
It is quiet
Yet I long for the water
And all of its chaos
All of its pride
Take me, even in the isolation
So that I may join its escapade

IV

We Turn to Beasts

HURT

Scratching on the surface
Dried tears and fresh scabs
From breaking me in
You pour from the chalice but never swallow
Spilling red as you close the curtains
Monopolising on my misery
Counting seconds like dimes
My brain resting on my sleeve
Since my heart fell out

OIL ON FEATHERS

Oil on my feathers
I am beaten
Bested
Sinking to the bottom
I cannot swim
I cannot fly

BLOOD IN THE WATER

The teeth sink in
Erupting my skin
Mixing blood into the water
Painting the sea
With pain's ink

LITTLE SERPENT

Come now, bite into me
Your little serpent, coiled around your open palm
For you have a hold of me
And I cannot shake your grasp
Flowers might wither, but I will withstand
So water me in your garden
And make me your furniture
So that I can bloom in your arms
Feed me to the insects
And nurture our soil
For I am alive
And fuelling this pyre

INSTINCT

Written in my skull are words I cannot see
They're carved into bone and tendon
They sing into my blood and grasp onto my heart
Parasitic, they feed on my wit and emboss my brain
My lungs are filled with pheromone
I breathe you in
I dilate
Every conversation becomes a dance
Played out by our tongues
We entwine
Relapsing into our instincts
My body begs
It hungers and yearns
Take me, for I am nothing
Sense trembles on the brink
As you watch me unfold
Repose and reform
Cutting through these wires
Unveiling your core
I am yours

DREAMER'S DISEASE

The feet walk while they dream of dancing
The mouth whispers while it yearns to sing
And the hands clench tightly
If only to crawl
If only to climb

TEETH

It stirs in my fibres
Waiting for you to sink your teeth
Into every part of me
I am your prey
I go willingly
Into the dark
Into the flames
Taunt me ripe
Sharpen your fangs
Rip me apart and feast on my needs
For in this moment, you are everything

MURDER

They utter above
Watching the worms below
A black curtain over the rooftops
Beckoning
And I am among them

HUNGER

Tremble in the shadow
Waiting for the moment
To cover you in attention
For the hit of dopamine
Fangs sharp and mind sharper
Feels like lightning in the limelight
Fake smile, fake friends
They bow to you
Behold the empty crown
Upon the head you hold
Fit for a jester
Fit for the dirt

DON'T FORGET TO SMILE

Vile
While they're selling death to you
Dressed up in cigarettes and ethanol
And trading your face to basement dwellers
Criminal tendencies fuelled in spending sprees
Happiness is the weekend
And political campaigns
Free totes and water bottles
Branded with fascists and control
Sleeping with racism
You are all alone
I said
Smile for the camera
And every man who hates you
Feeding the ego and the rich
With every narcotic and dollar bill

MUTATE

I am not alone
I have a hundred friends
Wrapped around my brain
They told me everything about you
When my arms were restrained

They talk to me violently
Pressing on my veins
Rupturing my mind
Until I emerge again

Cupping my cortex
Questioning my reign
But, I swear, they all love me
As long as I obey

SCALES

How I yearn for you from these aching depths
Water in my eyes, and dirt on my skin
I watch you, filling my mouth with metaphors
Words I'd never heard
I am a beast
But I love all the same
How do I tell my heart that I cannot hold your hand
When I cannot even walk?

The water keeps me quiet when my chest is screaming
Fists gripped to shells and calamity
Wrapped up in diatoms and melancholy
I am alone
But I hate all the same
That I cannot drown
How do I tell my heart that I cannot sing
When I cannot even talk?

EMULSION

I saw the darkness in you
Permeating the air around your head
You left it to fester in your cells
Dripping into holy water
By the grace of your own heart
It floated on the surface
Far enough for me to see
The shimmer of its reach
Black and gold
Weaving in the sunlight
A gesture of your arrogance

GLITCH

A glitch in the system
They call it melancholy
Chasing prescriptions
With dreamer's folly

OSMOSIS

Life is a storm, and I am a cloud
Chasing myself into the ether
I land on dreams and memories
Long since passed, long since forgotten

TAIPAN

Breaking down every word you said
Shedding the weight of your hate
Then using my skin as a blanket
I am a serpent
I am a devourer
I comfort myself in the mess
Unhinge my jaw
Swallowing everything
My mouth filled with blood
Forever I gorge
I am the blade
Rip off the gauze
I see red when you talk
How are you so grotesque
Where every no becomes a yes
How is every woman your prey
As a fucking pest
Tonight I tear you apart
Mourn
You are an afterthought

EUDAEMON

I sat in shame, but you ascended me
A collection of stories that you fit together
Into a silhouette
Tending to me
And all of my scars
Kintsugi
You cut the puppet strings
That propped me up in distant places
My veins are vibrant
My wrath subsided
You honour me
In your warmest embrace

HOLLOW

And what would the point be
In wearing this crown
If I am to be alone?
The space by my side is empty
Not even a shadow lay resting
I am to taste true abandonment
For on the shore, I am nothing
Swept up by a sense of loss
I lay in wake
Watching you walk away
I cannot scream your name
But I stay, listening to your footsteps
They grow quiet
As the waves grow deafening
And I am destined for the seabed

FREAQUE

Hold yourself over me
And invade my hungering mind
I am in need
I am a lock and only you have the key
Hushed in my humbleness
With something sinister underneath
Please
Make me feel alive
Set me free
With your clenched hands
Radiating dominance

CREATURE

I relished you from a distance
In the hopes your eyes would find me
And I would hide
But they found me
And took everything
They cut off my fins
Throwing my body back to the sea
Watching me sink
Silently dying
Cries to the empty ocean floor
Suffering in isolation
With nothing but rock and my rotting body
Comforting me in the very end

ASPHYXIATE

If I meant nothing at all
Would you still hold me over your head
Wrap me in your anger
And suffocate the voices
They're calling your name
Like your own brand of psychosis
Packaged in my screams
And underneath my clothes
Dissolved in spit and lesions
You give and I must take

V

Haunted House

FLESH

Wrap me in your arms
With the warmest parts of your heart
Cocooned in love
My flesh is undone

INSANE

The Devil comes knocking
On the doors painted in God's name
Who gets a seat at the table
When the Sinners look like Saints

You asked the mirror if you're pretty
Through clenched fists and gritted teeth
May insanity take the world
Before all of your grief

GRAVEYARD SHIFT

The corporate noose clenches around your throat
You grind and you grind
In the hopes you will have chiselled a masterpiece
An ice sculptor of hope, of ambition
But all you have created
Is a monument of folly
Full of cracks
Full of lies
Fuelled by the vending machine
Of false promises
Throwing coal into the furnace
That powers the freight train to your demise

SKELETON

Mother forgive me
I fell in love with a monster
When I knocked they let me in
I didn't mean to claim another skeleton

HORROR SHOW

Televised, terrorised
Advised to stay inside
To rot away like good soldiers
Clapping for better days
While the lands blossom
Away from human noise
While bodies pile
And hospital beds become graves
Accept your fate
It is not the bread we break
But our spirit, as a Nation
Comply
"To halt the spread of this disease"

SICK

I told them I was sick
So they showed me the doctors
I told them I was sick
So they showed me the martyrs
They told me I was sick
So they lobotomised
Bedlam bitch
Not quite alive, not quite fixed

BONES

Write your name in my bones
And I'll sail on my dreams
To the garden of granite and epilogues
Where I'll wait for you
I'm ready for my peace
And to detach from my skin
Show me love
Like you never did before
Let me see your heart burst
Trap me in the dirt
And watch the grass grow
Water it with your tears
And feed it with your eulogy

KNIFE DANCE

Stitch me up when I fall back down
I brought a gun to the knife dance
They pranced around me like dragonflies

And when they cried out
I let loose on the world
My bullets of ambition

BODIES

When you stepped over bodies
Stacked up in the streets
The lost and the lonely
Convulsing from the realisation
That they are forgotten
Did you ask their names
And hear their rasps
Or was it a race to the broadcast
The terrorised being televised
Narration through silver screens

SLEEPWALKING

When I look at you I see stars
Butterflies dance around my chest
And my hands start to sweat
I feel like my heart is encased in the softest sheets
Warm
Cherished
And I can sing out of tune
Because you'll still want to hear it
And I can dance with two left feet
Because you'll fall down with me
You'll play your guitar, and I'll hum along
And we'll laugh so hard we'll cry
Thinking about the good times
When you'd hold me in the ocean
As the sun set in front of us
When you'd spin me round
Just to kiss me in the street
For all to see
And that would be our story
We'd tell the world
If they ask us
How we met
How we fell in love

HAUNTING

I move around you, within the walls
Your breath
Your restraint
You come for me
But I am a ghost
Haunting these halls
Surrounding you
Tracing my thirst
My urge
My greed
Into the night
Where we entwine
And give in to our desire

REVERSE RUSSIAN ROULETTE

Load up the chamber
Keep one clear
It's like Russian Roulette
Except a lot more fear
I can't see past the barrel
Through smoke and false ego
Am I the reaper or the Devil
Chasing placebo

BASEMENT

Your mind is in the gutter
Mine is in the basement
You're chasing the pipelines
I'm chasing the pavement
Shall we connect the dots
And harvest what remains
All that was lost
In our final statements

NOVOCAINE

If I must suffer then I will a thousand times
Until my breath leaves my lungs
Until I forget my own name
I will look for you
At the bottom of every bottle
At the end of every rope
I will listen to the evening winds
At dawn, at the Golden Hour
For your voice beckoning me
And take my place by your side
But until then
I agonise
I repent
I wait
I try again

GHOSTS

Let's dance 'til the dawn
On the cobbled floor
Until the sun comes up
Let's be ghosts in the graveyard
Reminiscing about the pain
And the joy
Of this thing called life

BALLROOM

So we'll parade these halls for eternity
Laced in black and forlornness
Awaiting our demise
With stitched up hands

RUST

You are the saddest song I ever heard
The unbound book
The dug up grave
You are the letters rubbed from a sign
The lost hope
The American Dream
You are the rust on an otherwise perfect machine
The oil stains
The catharsis
You are the last bite after gorging
The discomfort
The unappeal

You are the healthcare bill
You are the processed food in everyone's meal

ALTER

If the Devil came to Kansas
Would you build your house
Where the dust coats your lungs
And the fires burn green
Would you stay to feed the flame
Offer words to the alter
Disembodied advocation
To appease the obscene

BED MONSTER

Don't fear the night
It has its own symphony
You draw the knife
Checking twice
From underneath the sheets

Disgusting altercations
Abrasions of your own kind
Trauma brings infections
Of already troubled minds

VAMPIRE

I feel it coursing in your system
Like a twisted sedation
Bare your skin and I'll begin
Our obscene celebrations
I move in hushed whispers
Terrorising your heartbeat
My dear, forgive my sins
You look good enough to eat

ALONE

My sleep paralysis has become my favourite past time
At least then
I am not alone

NEVERMORE

I will no longer be;

Receptionist
Therapist
Publicist
Exhibitionist

Nurse
Teacher
Chef
Housekeeper

Quiet
Silent
Shy
Violent

I have become the Leviathan

And you are the weak

SEND IN THE CLOWNS

My mind is a circus
Isn't that what you wanted
Walking along your tightrope
Destined to be haunted
Always on edge
Cursed in your trope
A freak in your way
A freak in your show

DOWNPOUR

Torrential rain
When the window is broken
It leaves a stain, a crashing spray
Over our half-filled heads
Give me a sign
That the waters are coming
I wait for their pull
While I'm drowning out your noise
With the flood and the rain
Pull out my vein
So that I might wash away
Marks on these brittle hands
Just like the waves will take me
Temper emerges
In cherished disorder

PIG

Consume
And let it be a lesson to you
Disease served on silver platters
Digesting the bad news
Countries running on Xanax
Meat hooks controlled by maniacs
Slicing off your sanity
One procedure at a time
Hot and fresh
Advertisement for the afterlife
Each pound of flesh
Mapped out trauma in muscle segments
Red, white, and sue
Another spoiled pig
Blocking your view

ESCAPE ROOM

Funny how we pay for the scabs someone else made
We bandage up the wounds
That come calling in the night
Now my dreams offer no respite
Bodies in the hazard bin
Doctors, demented hat tricks
I break through and I hate you

THE DEAD WILL MARCH

Bring your stakes, bring your cross
You'll be left out with the moss
Marching to your grave
On falsehoods and false Gods
There's not enough dirt
For all of us

MAUSOLEUM

Residing in the death pit of our demise
My weary soul finally rests
How long were you holding on
To the strings of my life
I resign
With a bruised tongue
And brittle bones
Let this be my elegy
My abdication
That I will never return
To your closet of corpses
With lies wrapped up in lace
And whispers for screams

POLTERGEIST

I go where I please
Yet she's there and she feeds
I savour every thought of her
The imperfect and the nameless
She's the tremble on my lips
A storm to be reckoned with
Her voice burns on my brain
Haunting me in other ways
I can't restrain
Focus fractured in her gaze
Do I risk the heart I've only known to break
For the sake of her caress
She is the heiress
She smells like gold
With roses for pheromones
She tastes like blood and honey
Sins served cold
She could burn down the whole world
All for the fun of it
Yet she would still follow me
Deep into the night

CO-CANE HILL

Fall down
And medicate your madness
There's no pity in this world
For your kind of sadness
Burn it down, burn it down
Six feet under ground
Carnival of lunatics
Every bombshell, every tick
Strike the match
With your best pose
To make them think they've cured you
Your own false anecdote
Howell at the moon
You pray without a cross
Aversos compono animos

GRAVESTONE ETIQUETTE

Who knew graves had ghosts
Who knew existence was voluntary
There's sulphur on my lips
Tasteless like your sodomy
Who told you to trace me
Chase me in the dark
Taking everything I have
Just to cut me down
And tear me apart
Can you feel it
The last pumps of adrenaline
Reach the tips of my hands
Dare me to fight
Dare me to fly

THERAPY

I watch you watching me
A taste to terrorise
All of my demons are in the room
You tap them on the shoulder
Asking their origin
But they only smile
I know you're trying to help
You try writing it down
But you're trapped in here with me
Not the other way round

VI

Φωσφόρος

CRADLE

Your scent lingers on my fabrics
Your hair is silk, woven in my fingertips
I wake to your heartbeat and warming kisses
They soothe my demons like morning coffee
I hear you peaceful
I feel you cradled to my breast
An exchange of comfort, silently hanging between our heads
I would hold the world up so you could walk under it
For I have never known love like this

BLACK WAX

We coalesce in the dark of night
Dripping wax over our wounds
Sewing our bodies together
With the strings of our hearts

We dance the dance of doves
A flickering candle light
A warmth within the cold
Subjects of each other's gaze

Would you risk Hell with me
To hold hands in the fires
If it meant we'd be together
If it meant we weren't alone

DEUS

I wear these scars as a statement
Skin uniform, blood hits the pavement
I'm a swarm
I'm a storm
Hungry for some lies when I ate the truth
Callouses on my brain and powdered membranes
Trauma Queens in cult forums
Shooting reg flags out of t-shirt canons
Fast fashion faster lovers
Never satisfied, forever chasing testaments

EDEN

I wish to know the dance of your heart
The words on your tongue
To memorise each reverb
So that I may harmonise
And wrap myself around you
Ingest the forbidden fruit
And share, with you, God's consequence

ETERNITY

For eternity I would wait
To feel your fingers press on my skin
To melt into the sky
And in this moment
Forever never tasted so good

FORBIDDEN FRUIT

Cracks on my fingertips
Tell me, where are the fruits of our labour
But rotten on the ground
I walk to the well
To fill the pail
It never over-spills
And my cup remains empty

Who tends to your church
Your garden of Eden
Overrun with weeds and malice
Underneath your mask
Sits a milquetoast man
Pressing for perfection
With an iron rod and a crown of thorns

I understand now
That I am a disciple
Serving your hunger
A mindless machine
Whipped into submission
A lasso laced in lies
Cutting off my brain

I must find my own mercy
For none rests in these four walls
The sun shines through the drapes
But it offers no relief
I repent
Forgiveness rests only in my chest
But you're holding the stake

DOZER

Perverse in all the places God couldn't reach
And the Devil wished he could
Where the creatures crawl and sharpen teeth
And the spirits come to brawl
Guard dog of your nightmares
Forged in leather and nicotine
Cigarette smoke echoing fog
Reiterating your fever dreams

THOUGHTS AND PRAYERS

And have you got your ever after
Feeding off the weak
And when you've taken everything
What will you eat

ANVIL

Let me be your anvil
That forges the sword
I cut through the noise
I cut through the pain
I will be the drum
That sounds out the beating of your heart
I fall like embers in your eyes
As we ignite
As we shatter the wounds
That kept us in the dark
I have known you
In past lives
I feel it in my bones
I feel it in my soul
Etched into my fate
In this life and the next
I will wait for you
After the last ship sails
I will watch for your flag
And speak to the winds
To bring you safely back to me

PAIN

I know pain, for I have seen it
I know guilt, for I will bleed it
And when the Devil comes to tempt me
I will stand and make him plead it

BIOLUMINESCENCE

We've all got a God
Sometimes they're in a barrel
Parading in pill packets and shot glasses
Blood turns to wine
And tears to tequila
Yet we fill ourselves
With hope and harnessed confidence
That we will shine brighter
Despite the pagans
And the ill-wishers
Who haunt our daydreams
In the form of small talk and come downs

THIS CHURCH

The maggots beg
While you break bread with the Devil
Pulverise the Holy Ghost
Capitalise on metal
Your palace of gold
Feeds into the ego
While the holy taint God
From the paws of the tyrant

HORNS

I see your demons
And you see mine
They tell each other stories
As they waltz in each other's company

CULTISTS

Holy Roller, come to parade
Tell them of their sins
Pews of the lost
A sea of faces, basking in false Sun
And rotting roods
Hearts tied to hymn books and picket fences
Perfect wives and perfect lives
Obeying tyrants, taken as Gospel
In the hopes of salvation
For their onslaught of sins

SERAPHIM

Do you dare enter my presence
With an arched back and raised brow
I see all that you are
I taste your pride, like burnt wood and rotten meat
The bridges you burned stick soot to your clothes
Staining you in your ego's shadow
You are not worthy
You are a fly, and I am a God

LOCUSTS

Like ink in the water, it birth only darkness
Erupting fatalities and soiled dreams
Wishes of flowers become nightmares of locusts
And so I wait
For the end of days

DESERT

I wither like flowers in the sun
Mirages of our deepest days
Yet I would follow you
To the ends of the Earth
And even more
Dancing with the heat stroke
If you need me, I will appear
And lead you to paradise
And if you leave
I will tread eternity alone
Singing your name
With a knife in my heart
You are the colours in my clothes
The fresh air in my lungs
The definition of perfect
That vibrates to my bones

Fin.

Acknowledgements

Thank you to my family for always believing in me, and all of my wacky ideas. You have always supported me, and it's because of you that I have achieved so much. Nothing will ever be great enough to return the favours. The many, many, favours.

Thank you to my old boss E. Townsend who gave me my first tarot card deck, and a book that helped with writing novels. Even then you were supportive of everyone who had a dream. It was motivating and I felt too bad to write in it. But you showed me the meaning of "firm but fair" and being a "powerhouse".

Thank you to my Dragonfly. Our hive mind brought the book's art to life, and made it possible. It's better than I could have imagined. You always made me feel good about doing something scary.

To my Nan and Granddad, who are no longer in this realm. There's a lot that I wish I could tell you, and some of it would probably make you laugh. Thanks for always sitting me in front of horror movies that I was definitely too young to watch as a kid, and for baking with me. I still think about sitting in the back room playing with Lego, when you got your new furniture for the front room, and decorating the Christmas tree with you every year. Sorry I "got too old" (busy) to do it, but the foil garlands you put up, that had years of cigarette smoke clinging to them, are permanently imprinted into my brain. Love you more than chips.

Tom (Great Granddad). Thanks for everything you did in your later years. You were always so grateful for our company. I'd have loved to tell you all about my 2024 trip to Edinburgh. Can't believe it took me that long to go. Rest easy.

Finally, I'd just like to acknowledge the amazing world around us - so full and vibrant. Take the time to go and look at some bugs or walk through the woods. Breathe unpolluted air, and look at the sky. You won't regret it.

<u>About the Author</u>

Courtney W is a music industry professional that works closely with artists, event organisers, and multiple areas of the creative industries. Her role often dips into aspects of mental health and diversity. Her passion for music started at a young age, being influenced by rock music. Later, she discovered metal at the age of 13 . This sparked her creativity in lyricism, and developing that form of writing. She entered the American Songwriter Lyric Contest in 2024.

Born in the UK, Courtney published *"Arachnid"* as her first published work; a collection of free verse poetry that dips into all forms of human emotion, showcasing her raw and emotive writing style.

Arachnid

www.ingramcontent.com/pod-product-compliance
Lightning Source LLC
Chambersburg PA
CBHW011935050726
47590CB00011B/3304